MAYER SMITH

Her Secret Fortune, His Only Heart

First edition

This book was professionally typeset on Reedsy.
Find out more at reedsy.com

Contents

One

Secret Inheritance

Lila Montgomery had always been a woman of restraint, her life neatly compartmentalized, each moment carefully curated. She prided herself on her independence, built from years of self-reliance. Nothing had ever come easy, but she'd worked hard to shape the life she had, a life in which the chaos of fortune had no place. Or so she thought.

It was a Tuesday when the letter arrived, simple, unremarkable, and sealed with an emblem she had never seen before. The crisp white envelope sat in the corner of her desk like an ominous reminder that something was about to change. She had been buried in her usual tasks, the mundane routine of her small but successful interior design business, when her eyes caught the unfamiliar crest embossed on the front of the envelope. She reached for it with a sense of unease, her fingers trembling ever so slightly as she sliced it open.

Inside, there was a single sheet of thick, cream-colored paper, folded precisely in half. The writing was elegant, scripted in a bold hand that almost seemed too deliberate, too neat to belong to anyone she knew.

Dear Ms. Montgomery,

I hope this letter finds you well. I write to you in a matter of great importance regarding the estate of your late aunt, Matilda Graves. As the executor of her will, it is my duty to inform you of a significant inheritance that has been bequeathed to you. Please contact my office at your earliest convenience to arrange for the reading of the will and the distribution of the assets.

Yours sincerely,

Harold Caldwell
  Attorney at Law

The words blurred before her eyes as she read them again. Her aunt, Matilda, had passed away six months ago. It hadn't been a surprise; Aunt Matilda had lived a full life, marked by eccentricities and whispers. She was a woman of mystery, a figure that had always been a shadow in Lila's life. They had not been close, though Lila remembered the faint scent of jasmine that seemed to follow her aunt like an aura. As a child, she'd been fascinated by Matilda's stories, the way she spoke of faraway places and hidden treasures, but those stories were always more fantasy than reality. Or so Lila had thought.

Inheritance.

Lila let the word hang in the air, the weight of it settling on her chest like a boulder. She had never expected anything from her aunt. In fact, she had assumed there would be little to inherit, given that Matilda had lived in a modest cottage on the outskirts of town and kept mostly to herself. But now, a hidden fortune? It was absurd. Her fingers clutched the letter tighter, crumpling the edges as the implications swirled in her mind.

A part of her wanted to ignore the letter, to discard it as some mistake, but the curiosity gnawed at her. What if it was true? What if her aunt had left her something? The thought of an inheritance was almost too surreal, and yet, Lila could not bring herself to dismiss it.

She dialed the number on the letter, the digits blurring together as her pulse quickened. The line rang twice before a woman's voice answered.

"Good afternoon, Caldwell & Associates. How may I assist you?"

"I'm calling about the letter I received," Lila began, her voice betraying the unease she felt. "It's regarding the inheritance of Matilda Graves. I—uh, I would like to arrange the reading of the will."

"Of course, Ms. Montgomery. We've been expecting your call. Mr. Caldwell will be happy to meet with you at your convenience. Would Thursday at 10 AM work?"

Lila nodded, though the woman on the other end of the line couldn't see her. "Yes, that works. Thank you."

As she hung up, her thoughts raced. What was this inheritance, and why had her aunt left it to her? The questions spiraled in her mind, each more pressing than the last. She wasn't even sure if she wanted anything to do with it. What if it changed everything?

But what if it didn't?

Lila hadn't had much in her life that was given to her. Everything she had now, the modest home, the business that was just starting to find its footing, had been earned through sheer determination. She had always prided herself on making her own way, and this inheritance, this mysterious fortune, felt like something that didn't belong in her world. But then again, neither did the feeling of loneliness that clung to her at night, the quiet emptiness that sometimes consumed her when she turned off the lights.

The meeting was set for Thursday, and in the days that followed, Lila couldn't shake the thought of what awaited her. The calm routine of her life had been irrevocably altered, and now, it seemed, there was no going back.

—-

Thursday morning arrived, and Lila stood outside the stately building where Caldwell & Associates was located, her breath visible in the cold air. The building was imposing, the kind of place where secrets were kept in leather-bound books and things of importance were discussed behind closed doors. The tall glass windows gleamed in the early light, and the sound of the bustling city around her felt muted, as if the world itself had quieted in anticipation of whatever was about to unfold.

Inside, the office was sleek and modern, with dark wood paneling and soft leather chairs that made Lila feel out of place. She was ushered into a small conference room, where an older man, tall with graying hair and a sharp suit, stood to greet her.

"Ms. Montgomery," he said with a nod. "It's a pleasure to meet you. I'm Harold Caldwell."

Lila shook his hand, trying to steady her nerves. "Thank you for meeting with me, Mr. Caldwell."

"Of course. Please, take a seat," he gestured to the chair across from him. As she sat, he began to flip through the papers in front of him, his movements deliberate and precise. There was something calculating about him, something that made Lila uncomfortable, but she couldn't place her finger on why.

Caldwell cleared his throat. "As you know, your aunt Matilda was a private woman, and her will was kept under lock and key until now. She had… considerable assets that she left behind, but her instructions were very clear. You, Ms. Montgomery, are the sole beneficiary of her estate."

Lila's breath caught in her throat. "I'm the sole beneficiary?"

"Yes," he said, his voice steady, as if he had delivered this news countless times before. "Your aunt left behind a fortune, and it's yours now. It is my responsibility to see that you understand what you've inherited and what that means for your future."

"Fortune?" Lila whispered, the word unfamiliar on her tongue. "But how? My aunt… she didn't seem like someone who would have—"

"Your aunt was a woman of many talents and interests," Caldwell interrupted, a glint of something she couldn't quite interpret flashing in his eyes. "She was very well-versed in investments, and there are assets that she accumulated in various forms—real estate, stocks, precious metals, and, I believe, some rare artifacts."

Lila felt as though the room was spinning. "What am I supposed to do with all of this?" she asked, her voice shaky. "I—this is too much. I'm not prepared for this kind of responsibility."

Caldwell leaned back in his chair, studying her with an unreadable expression. "There is more to it, Ms. Montgomery. Much more. Your aunt's estate is not only valuable, but it is also shrouded in secrecy. There are… conditions attached to your inheritance. You must tread carefully."

The words hung in the air like a warning. Lila's heart raced as she processed the gravity of what Caldwell had just said. There was something more, something she hadn't been prepared for. The fortune she had inherited might just come with a price—one that could cost her far more than money.

As the meeting drew to a close, Lila left the office with a growing sense of dread. The secrets her aunt had kept, the legacy of wealth, and the conditions tied to it were only the beginning. In the days to come, Lila would come to realize that uncovering the truth would unravel her entire world.

Two

Deception

Lila Montgomery had always been good at hiding things. As a child, she'd hidden her journals from prying eyes, careful not to let anyone discover the vulnerable thoughts she poured onto their pages. As an adult, she'd learned to hide her dreams, her deepest desires, afraid that sharing them would invite ridicule or disappointment. But the secret she had carried for the last week was unlike any other.

The inheritance.

It was heavy, too heavy to carry without consequences, and it had started to change the way she viewed the world around her. She had kept it hidden from everyone, including her closest friends, as though shielding herself from the very thing that could alter her entire life. But each time she woke up in the morning, the weight of it was there, pressing down on her chest like a physical force. It was as if her aunt's fortune had invaded her soul, and now she was trapped between the life she had built and the one she was being forced to embrace.

It wasn't just the money, though that alone was enough to unsettle her. It was the promise of a life she hadn't expected—one that seemed like a fairy tale at first glance, but whose dark undercurrents she couldn't ignore. The rare artifacts, the precious metals, the properties—each piece of the inheritance was a puzzle in itself. What had Matilda left her? And more importantly, why? Why had she chosen Lila as the sole beneficiary, a woman with no experience in such matters, someone who had always managed to get by with modest means?

For days, Lila barely slept, her mind racing with the possibilities. She tried to keep herself busy—working on a new design project for a local restaurant, meeting with contractors, and handling the endless flow of emails and phone calls that came with running her business. But no matter how hard she tried to focus, her thoughts kept returning to the same question: What did it all mean?

She had gone over the details of her aunt's will in her head over and over again. The words were etched into her memory now. There were instructions, yes, but they were vague—cryptic even. "You must follow the path Matilda has set for you," the will had stated. "Only then will you understand the full extent of what I leave behind." What path? What did she mean? Matilda was a woman who had never revealed much of herself to anyone, even to Lila, who had known her for years.

It wasn't like her aunt had been a recluse, but she had been… different. There had always been an air of mystery surrounding her. Lila remembered when she was a little girl, visiting her aunt's cottage on the outskirts of town. Matilda's home was like something out of a fairy tale, with its ivy-covered walls and dark wooden beams. There were no flowers in the garden— just herbs and plants that Lila had never seen before. And inside the house, the atmosphere was thick with the smell of incense and old books. Her aunt always had strange trinkets scattered around—objects that seemed to hold significance, but were never explained. Lila had always assumed they were just eccentricities, but now, with the inheritance in her hands, she wasn't so sure.

It was after the meeting with Harold Caldwell, the executor of the will, that the first crack appeared in her carefully constructed life. He had mentioned the conditions of the inheritance, but they hadn't been detailed. Instead, he had spoken in riddles, as if daring her to uncover the truth for herself. And what was worse—he had made it clear that there were things about the estate that must be kept secret. He had said it in a way that made it sound like her ignorance was both a blessing and a curse.

Lila had left his office feeling unsettled, as though the ground beneath her was slowly eroding, leaving her unsure of where to stand. The inheritance was not just a fortune—it was a trap. She could feel it in her bones, this sense of being pulled into something much larger than herself. But what could she do? The money was real. The artifacts were real. The estate was real. And it had been left to her.

But then, she realized something else: she had been hiding, even before the inheritance. Hiding from herself, hiding from the truth. She had spent her entire life afraid of stepping into the unknown, always choosing the safer route. But now, the unknown was thrust upon her, and there was no turning back. She couldn't un-know what she had learned in that cold, sterile office. She couldn't un-hear the name of her aunt's lawyer, Harold Caldwell, or the strange warning he had given her. This inheritance, whatever it was, was not something she had asked for, but now it was hers, and she couldn't just walk away from it.

—-

The following days passed in a blur. Lila kept to herself, rarely answering calls or responding to messages. She found it easier to be alone, to retreat into the sanctuary of her home, where she could think in peace. But even in the silence, the weight of the inheritance loomed over her.

On Friday, she received a call that would shatter the fragile peace she had built in her mind.

"Lila," a voice said, sharp and insistent. "This is Damon Clarke. I need to speak with you."

Damon was one of her closest friends, someone she had known since high school. He was a journalist, a writer who had a way with words that made even the dullest topics seem interesting. She had always admired his ability to find stories where others saw only dust and rubble. But now, his tone was different, more urgent than she had ever heard it before.

"What's going on?" she asked, her voice betraying her anxiety.

"I've been hearing things," Damon continued, his voice low. "About your aunt. About her business. Lila, I think there's something you're not telling me."

Lila's heart skipped a beat. Damon's words hit her like a freight train. Her mind raced—what could he possibly know? She had kept her aunt's secret well hidden. No one knew about the inheritance, no one knew about the strange details in the will. How could he possibly know?

"What do you mean?" she asked, trying to keep her voice steady, though the unease was growing rapidly inside her.

"I don't know how to explain this, but there's been some chatter, Lila," Damon said. "People are talking about your aunt's death and what she left behind. They say there's more to the story, something that doesn't add up. Someone's been digging around, and I don't like where this is going."

The blood drained from her face. Someone's been digging around?

Lila had assumed the only people who knew about her aunt's estate were Harold Caldwell and a few distant relatives. But now, Damon's words sent a chill down her spine. Someone else was involved. Someone who had found out about the inheritance, and was trying to piece together what Matilda had left behind.

"I need to see you," Damon said. "Tonight. We need to talk."

Lila didn't respond right away. Her mind was spinning, the implications of Damon's words too overwhelming to process. She had no choice but to meet with him. The pieces were starting to fall into place, but what she was seeing didn't make sense. There was something hidden beneath the surface of this inheritance, something she hadn't yet uncovered.

She agreed to meet him at a local café later that evening, her thoughts racing the entire way there. What had Damon discovered? Who else knew? And most importantly, what kind of world had her aunt been involved in that could be dangerous enough to draw attention?

As she walked into the café, she spotted Damon sitting at a corner table, his brow furrowed in concentration. His expression softened when he saw her, but Lila could sense the tension in his body, the way he was on edge.

"What's going on, Damon?" she asked, her voice trembling despite her efforts to sound composed.

Damon leaned forward, his voice barely a whisper. "Lila, there's something you don't know. Something about your aunt's past. And I think you're in danger."

Three

New Neighbor

Lila sat in her small kitchen, the early morning light streaming through the window, casting a soft glow on the cluttered countertop. She hadn't slept much the night before, her mind still reeling from the conversation with Damon. The warning he'd given her echoed in her thoughts: "You're in danger." She hadn't had the chance to process what that meant, but now, more than ever, she felt a weight pressing on her shoulders. She needed answers, and time was running out.

Her fingers wrapped around her coffee mug, the warmth doing little to settle the unease that had become a constant companion. With a deep breath, she set the mug down and pulled herself together. She couldn't afford to fall apart now, not when there was so much at stake. The inheritance, the secrets of her aunt, and the looming threat that seemed to be drawing closer by the day. But there was another thought, a new one, that had been taking root in her mind. She couldn't ignore it.

The new neighbor.

Lila had noticed him moving in a few days ago, the young man with the messy dark hair and the eyes that seemed to see everything. He had arrived with a truck full of boxes and a quiet air of mystery. She had watched him from her living room window, her gaze lingering on him longer than she cared to admit. There was something about him that made her uneasy, but also something that pulled at her curiosity. The way he moved, the way he carried himself—it was like he was hiding something, just like she was.

The knock on her door came as a surprise, sharp and sudden, pulling her from her thoughts. Lila hesitated for only a moment before walking across the room. She wasn't expecting anyone, not after the whirlwind of the past week. Her hand reached for the doorknob, but before she could open it, the door swung open, and standing there was the man she had been trying not to think about.

"Hi, Lila," he said, his voice smooth and friendly, though his eyes held a glimmer of something else—something that made her heart skip a beat. "I'm your new neighbor, Nick Holloway. I just moved in next door."

Lila blinked, momentarily taken aback by his sudden appearance. She hadn't expected him to show up at her door so soon, but now that he was here, she couldn't help but feel a strange sense of inevitability. It was as if their paths were destined to cross, whether she wanted it or not.

"Oh," Lila said, forcing a smile, though she couldn't hide the flicker of suspicion in her eyes. "I didn't realize anyone had moved in next door. It's nice to meet you, Nick."

Nick flashed a grin that could melt any suspicion in an instant, but there was something about that smile that felt a little too practiced, like it was hiding something beneath the surface. "I just got in yesterday," he said, stepping back slightly, as if giving her space. "I wanted to introduce myself. You know, be a good neighbor. I'm sure you'd like to know who's living next door."

Lila nodded, trying to mask the tension that was slowly building inside her. "I appreciate that," she said. "Are you settling in okay?"

"Getting there," Nick replied with a shrug. "Still unpacking, but it's a start. I thought maybe I could invite you over for coffee sometime. You know, get to know each other better. I'm sure you're busy, but if you're free, it would be nice to chat."

Lila's heart raced, her mind spinning with possibilities. It wasn't unusual for neighbors to be friendly, but there was something about Nick's offer that felt off. It wasn't just his sudden appearance or the way he seemed too eager to make her acquaintance—it was the fact that, for the first time in days, Lila felt a surge of something else: a sense of danger.

Her instincts were telling her to keep her distance, but she couldn't shake the feeling that she needed to know more about this man. Could he be connected to the strange events surrounding her aunt's inheritance? Could he be the one Damon had warned her about? Or was he just another person looking for a friendly conversation in an otherwise quiet neighborhood?

"Sure," Lila said, her voice steady despite the storm brewing inside her. "Coffee sounds nice. I'll stop by later today. I have a few things to take care of this morning, but I'll come by after lunch."

Nick's smile widened, and for a moment, he looked almost too pleased, as if he had won some small victory. "I'll be looking forward to it," he said, before turning and walking down the porch steps toward his house next door.

Lila watched him go, her eyes narrowing slightly as he disappeared into the house. Something about him unsettled her, but she couldn't quite figure out what. Was it his charm? His calm demeanor? Or was it the fact that she couldn't shake the feeling that he knew more about her life than he was letting on?

As she closed the door behind her and leaned against it, Lila tried to ignore the unsettling thoughts swirling in her mind. She had too much to deal with already—too many questions about the inheritance, too many shadows lurking in the corners of her life. She didn't have the luxury of focusing on a new neighbor. Yet, somehow, it felt like Nick's arrival couldn't have been more timely. Or more suspicious.

—-

Lila found herself at Nick's doorstep a few hours later, her heart pounding in her chest. She had tried to dismiss the strange feeling, but it clung to her, growing stronger with every step she took toward his house. She had no reason to be afraid, not really. He was just a neighbor. But something told her that meeting him wasn't going to be as simple as she'd hoped.

Nick answered the door almost immediately, as if he had been waiting for her. His smile was warm, genuine even, but Lila couldn't shake the sense that he was watching her closely, as if trying to read her every move. She forced a smile in return, stepping into the house with him.

The interior of his home was surprisingly sparse, with only a few boxes scattered around, most of them unopened. There were no personal touches, no pictures on the walls, no signs of a life lived. It was clean, almost too clean, as if he hadn't truly settled in yet—or perhaps had never planned to. Lila couldn't help but notice the subtle tension in the air, the feeling that something wasn't quite right.

"Can I get you anything?" Nick asked, motioning toward the kitchen. "Coffee, tea, or something stronger?"

"Coffee would be fine," Lila said, trying to shake off the unease that threatened to overtake her.

As Nick turned to prepare the coffee, Lila glanced around the room. There was something about the space that made her feel like an intruder. The walls, the furniture, everything felt temporary, as if he had just arrived and wasn't sure if he was staying. But why would someone who had just moved in be so… guarded? She couldn't place it, but she felt like she was missing something important.

Nick returned with two cups of coffee, handing one to her as he sat across from her at the small table. The silence between them was thick, and for a moment, Lila felt like she was trapped in a game she didn't understand.

"So, Lila," Nick said, leaning forward slightly. "Tell me about yourself. What do you do around here? I mean, I'm still learning the ropes of the neighborhood, but you seem like someone who knows the area well."

Lila took a slow sip of her coffee, trying to focus on the conversation, but her thoughts kept drifting back to the inheritance, to the warning Damon had given her. She couldn't help but wonder if Nick knew about her aunt, about Matilda's strange legacy. Was he playing a part in something larger, something darker? She had no proof, no evidence, just a gut feeling that he was hiding something.

"I run a small business," she said cautiously, deciding to keep the conversation light. "Interior design. I've been working on a few projects recently, mostly local stuff."

"Sounds interesting," Nick said, nodding, but his eyes never left her face, as if he was studying her. "And how long have you been in the area?"

Lila hesitated. "A few years now. It's quiet, you know? Nice place to settle down."

Nick smiled again, but this time, there was something different about it. Something that made her feel even more like she was being watched. "I'm sure it is," he said softly. "But sometimes, even in the quietest places, things aren't what they seem, aren't they?"

Lila froze, her heart pounding in her chest. His words were casual, but they sent a cold shiver down her spine. She wasn't sure what he meant, but she knew one thing for certain: Nick Holloway wasn't just her new neighbor. He was something far more dangerous. And she had just walked right into the heart of whatever dark secret he was hiding.

Four

Unlikely

L ila had spent the rest of the afternoon trying to regain some semblance of normalcy, but every attempt to return to her routine felt like a failed effort. The coffee with Nick had left her unsettled, his casual words echoing in her mind. The things he had said had seemed innocent at the time, but now that she was alone, they felt like pieces of a puzzle she wasn't ready to solve. Things aren't what they seem, he had said, his gaze never leaving hers. It was a statement too heavy for such a simple conversation. She had come into the meeting expecting pleasantries, but something far darker lingered beneath his charm.

Lila sat in her living room, trying to focus on the draft of a design proposal, but the words on the page refused to align. The memory of her conversation with Nick wouldn't let her concentrate. The way his eyes had followed her every move, the strange undertone in his voice, the subtle tension in his body—everything had felt too deliberate. Too calculated.

She glanced at her phone, the time reading 6:15 PM. She had half an hour before her evening meeting with Damon. They had agreed to meet at the small café in town, a place where the noise and bustle of the city allowed them to speak in relative privacy. Despite the chaos swirling around her, Lila had come to rely on Damon for stability. He was the only person who seemed to understand the magnitude of the inheritance, the strange weight of it. The only one who knew about her late aunt's fortune.

The more time Lila spent trying to unravel Matilda's secret, the more questions arose. Why had her aunt kept everything hidden? What had she been trying to protect her from? And why had she chosen Lila to inherit it all? Was it a gift, or was it a trap? With every passing moment, the answers felt further out of reach.

She arrived at the café a few minutes early, slipping into a corner booth. The low hum of conversations around her did little to mask the tension in the air. Lila's mind raced, still trying to make sense of her last meeting with Nick. He had seemed so normal, so charming, but now, in the quiet of the café, the suspicion gnawed at her, like an itch she couldn't scratch. What was he hiding? Why had he moved into her neighborhood, so close to her home? Was it a coincidence, or was there something more to his arrival?

Damon walked in just as she was losing herself in thought.

His familiar face, with its sharp features and casual, easy-going smile, offered a momentary relief from the storm of uncertainty swirling around her. He slid into the booth across from her, his expression immediately softening when he saw the tension in her face.

"Lila," Damon said, his voice low and comforting. "You look like you haven't slept in days."

She smiled weakly. "It's been… a strange week." Her fingers tapped nervously against the ceramic mug in front of her, the warm steam rising into the air. She wished she could put her thoughts into words, but she wasn't sure where to start. How could she explain everything that had been happening? The inheritance. Nick. The unsettling feeling that something far worse was coming.

"Tell me," Damon urged. "What's going on? You've been distant lately. Is it the inheritance?"

Lila took a deep breath, trying to steady her emotions. It was difficult to talk about. She wasn't sure if she should even be confiding in Damon, but there was no one else she trusted more. "Yes. And no," she said, the words catching in her throat. "I mean, I don't even know where to begin. There's more to it, Damon. More than I'm letting on."

Damon leaned forward, his eyes narrowing with concern. "You're scaring me, Lila. What are you saying?"

Lila's gaze flickered to the window, as if expecting someone to be watching them. She lowered her voice. "It's the neighbor. Nick. He's… he's hiding something, Damon. I don't know what it is, but there's something off about him. And then there's the inheritance… my aunt's estate. I thought it was just money and some property, but now, I'm not so sure."

Damon's brow furrowed as he processed her words. "You think Nick is involved in all of this?"

"I don't know," Lila whispered, feeling the weight of her thoughts. "But I can't shake the feeling that he knows more than he's letting on. He's… he's been too interested in me. In my life. And I don't think it's just about being a neighbor. It feels like he's looking for something."

Damon's expression hardened, a flash of something dark crossing his face. "You need to be careful, Lila. If there's one thing I know about people like that, it's that they don't just show up by chance. There's always a reason. And if he's linked to your aunt's estate… we need to find out why."

Lila nodded, her chest tightening at the thought. "I don't know what to do. I've barely had time to think straight. Everything's happening so fast, and I'm not sure I can trust anyone right now, not even myself."

Damon reached across the table, placing a reassuring hand over hers. "You can trust me. I'll help you figure this out. Whatever it is, we'll find the truth together."

For a brief moment, the weight on Lila's shoulders lightened.

Damon had always been her rock, the one person she could rely on. His unwavering support meant everything to her, especially now, when everything else felt uncertain.

Just as she was about to speak again, a figure approached the table, breaking their conversation. Lila looked up, and her breath caught in her throat.

Nick was standing there, a casual smile on his face, his eyes glinting with an unreadable expression. He looked like he belonged in the café, as if he had been coming here for years. But the moment he saw Lila's startled face, his smile faltered just slightly, before he quickly masked it with charm.

"Sorry to interrupt," he said smoothly. "I didn't expect to see you here, Lila. It's a small world, isn't it?" He turned his gaze to Damon, his smile widening. "And you must be Damon. I've heard a lot about you."

Lila's heart raced, and for a moment, she couldn't speak. She had no idea how Nick had found them, or why he was here. But there was something so calculated about his timing, so deliberate, that it made her skin crawl.

Damon didn't seem as taken aback, however. He gave Nick a small, polite smile. "Nice to meet you, Nick. What brings you by?"

Nick shrugged nonchalantly, taking a step closer. "Just thought I'd grab a coffee. Lila and I were talking earlier, and I thought I'd join her."

Lila felt the hairs on the back of her neck stand up. There was no way this was a coincidence. He had deliberately tracked her down, probably to keep an eye on her. But why? Why now, and why here?

"Well," Damon said, breaking the tension with his easy-going tone, "we were just wrapping up. I'm sure Lila wouldn't mind another coffee, though. I have to run some errands anyway."

Lila was grateful for Damon's quick thinking. She nodded quickly, though her heart was still pounding. As Damon stood up, he gave Nick a curt nod and walked toward the door.

"Nice meeting you, Nick," Damon said over his shoulder. "Take care, Lila."

Nick watched him leave with a polite smile, but his eyes followed Damon's every move with an intensity that made Lila uneasy. When the door closed behind Damon, Nick slid into the seat across from her, his movements smooth, almost predatory.

"Well," he said, leaning forward with a smile that didn't quite reach his eyes. "It looks like we have some time to ourselves, don't we?"

Lila stiffened, her mind racing. There was no way she could ignore the suspicion gnawing at her now. Nick's behavior was too calculated, too precise. The timing. The way he had inserted himself into her life, just when she was beginning to uncover the truth about her aunt's inheritance. She had no idea what game he was playing, but one thing was clear: whatever it was, it was far from over.

The calm, friendly exterior Nick had shown her before was slipping, and in its place, a darker, more dangerous version of him was emerging. Lila couldn't let her guard down now. She had no idea what he wanted, but she was determined to find out. And if she had to play his game to uncover the truth, then she would.

But as she looked into his eyes, she realized something that made her stomach drop. She wasn't the only one with secrets.

Nick Holloway had his own agenda. And Lila Montgomery was about to get tangled in it.

Five

Proposal

Lila's mind churned as she walked home from the café, each step heavier than the last. Nick's sudden appearance had sent a ripple through the fragile calm she had been clinging to. She hadn't expected him to show up at the café, especially not in the middle of a conversation with Damon. The timing had been far too perfect. Too orchestrated. Nick was not just some friendly neighbor trying to get to know her. There was something more to him, something lurking beneath the surface, and she wasn't sure how to navigate it.

Her thoughts returned to Damon. He had been her anchor for so long, the one person she could trust, but now she couldn't shake the feeling that she was losing grip on even that. She hadn't told him everything, not all the details about the inheritance, not all the strange warnings that had been floating through her mind. She couldn't afford to burden him with the weight of it all—not yet. But as the evening deepened, Lila realized that she could no longer ignore the feeling that the world around her was closing in. The inheritance was no longer just about money—it was about something far darker, something she hadn't even begun to understand.

Her phone buzzed in her pocket, pulling her from her spiraling thoughts. It was a text from Damon, as she'd expected.

"We need to talk. Meet me at the usual spot tomorrow. 10 AM."

Lila hesitated, her fingers hovering over the screen. The urgency in his message was palpable, but part of her didn't want to meet him. Not yet. Not when Nick was now part of the equation. What if he was involved in whatever was happening? What if everything they had been talking about, the inheritance, the danger, was all connected to him?

She sent a quick reply, agreeing to meet. No use in avoiding the inevitable.

—-

The next morning, Lila found herself standing outside the small café again, the morning air cool against her skin. It had rained earlier, and the streets were slick with fresh water, the smell of damp pavement clinging to the air. She walked into the café, scanning the room until her eyes locked on Damon, who was already seated at their usual corner booth, his back to the window.

Lila hesitated for just a moment before making her way over to him. His eyes softened when he saw her, but there was a tension in his posture that hadn't been there the day before. His hands were clasped tightly in front of him, the knuckles white from the pressure.

"Lila," Damon greeted her quietly, standing as she approached. "You're here earlier than I expected. We need to talk."

Lila took a seat, but her nerves were on edge. She hadn't told Damon about her suspicions regarding Nick. She wasn't sure if she should. But it seemed like the conversation was already heading in that direction. She could feel it in her bones.

"What's going on, Damon?" she asked, her voice barely above a whisper.

Damon looked around the café before leaning in, his eyes scanning the room as though checking for anyone who might be eavesdropping. "There's something I haven't told you. Something that's been bothering me since our last meeting."

Lila's heart skipped a beat. "What do you mean? What's going on?"

Damon took a deep breath before answering. "I've been doing some digging. Not just into your aunt's estate, but into everything surrounding it. I've heard rumors, Lila. About Matilda. About the people she was involved with. And it's not pretty. These people—they're dangerous. They've been keeping tabs on the estate, and I'm afraid they've noticed you."

Lila's breath caught in her throat. "What? Who are these people? What does this have to do with the inheritance?"

"I'm not sure yet," Damon admitted, his voice low, "but I'm starting to think Matilda wasn't just a quiet woman with an eccentric fortune. She was mixed up in something much bigger than we thought. And it's not just the money. It's the people. Whoever they are, they won't hesitate to do whatever it takes to get their hands on whatever Matilda left behind."

Lila's mind reeled as she processed his words. "So what do we do? I can't just walk away from this, Damon. I have no choice but to figure it out. But I don't know where to start."

Damon's eyes met hers, his expression filled with a mixture of concern and resolve. "We need to find out everything we can about your aunt's past. We need to go deeper, Lila. You're in danger, and I'm afraid the longer you wait, the worse it's going to get."

Lila's head spun with the implications of his words. "You're right," she said softly. "I can't ignore this any longer. But how? I don't even know where to begin. My aunt was always so secretive."

Damon's gaze hardened, his jaw tightening. "We'll start with Nick."

Lila blinked in surprise. "Nick? What does he have to do with any of this?"

Damon leaned in even closer, his voice barely above a whisper. "I've been watching him. There's something off about him. Something I don't trust. He knows more than he's letting on, and I think he's connected to the people who are after your aunt's estate."

Lila's heart raced as she absorbed Damon's words. Nick. She had suspected something wasn't right about him, but hearing Damon say it out loud made it real. Nick knows something. She had no proof, but the unease that had been growing inside her ever since their first meeting now had a name. It was Nick. He was the key. He was the one standing between her and the answers she desperately needed.

"What do you want me to do?" she asked, her voice trembling with a mix of fear and determination.

"I want you to get close to him," Damon said, his eyes fixed on hers. "You need to find out what he knows. I know it's risky, but it's the only way. If he's involved in this—if he's working with the people after the estate—we need to find out how deep this goes. And we need to do it before it's too late."

Lila's mind raced. She had no idea how she could get close to Nick without arousing suspicion. He was already watching her, tracking her every move. She had barely spoken to him, yet he seemed to be involved in every part of her life now. But there was no other choice. If Damon was right, if Nick really knew something, then she had to find out what it was.

"I'll do it," Lila said, her voice steady despite the chaos churning inside her. "I'll get close to him. I'll find out what he knows."

Damon looked at her, his expression filled with a mixture of admiration and concern. "Be careful, Lila. This is dangerous. If we're right about Nick, you won't be able to trust anything he says. You'll need to keep your guard up at all times."

Lila nodded, her resolve hardening. "I will. I won't let anything happen to me. I'll find the truth, Damon. No matter what."

As they sat there, the weight of their plan settled between them, a silent understanding passing in the air. This was the beginning of something much bigger than either of them could have predicted. The inheritance, the secrets, Nick—they were all pieces of a puzzle that Lila was now determined to solve. But the more she thought about it, the more she realized how much danger she was in. The people after her aunt's fortune weren't going to let her uncover the truth without a fight. And now, she was about to face them head-on.

With a final look at Damon, Lila stood up. "I'll be in touch," she said quietly.

As she walked away from the table, the weight of the decision hung heavy on her shoulders. She was diving headfirst into a dangerous game, and there was no going back. But she had made her choice. She would find out what Nick knew. And she would do whatever it took to protect herself—and the secrets that had been buried for so long.

Six

Secrets and Lies

The next few days passed in a blur for Lila. It felt like the world had shifted beneath her feet, tilting in ways she couldn't comprehend. Once a blessing, the inheritance now felt like a curse she couldn't shake. The more she learned, the more she realized how little she knew about her aunt's life. Matilda's hidden past seemed to stretch out before her like a dark maze, each turn promising more danger, more uncertainty.

But it wasn't just the inheritance that occupied her thoughts. It was Nick. He had wormed his way into her life, into her thoughts, and now Lila couldn't shake the feeling that he was watching her every move. She couldn't go a day without thinking about him, about his smooth words and unnerving gaze. Every time she looked out her window, she wondered if he was standing on the other side of the glass, waiting. She knew he was hiding something, but she had no idea what.

Lila had agreed to Damon's plan. She would get close to Nick. She would find out what he knew about her aunt's estate, about the people who were after it. But the more she thought about it, the more she realized how risky it was. She was playing a dangerous game, one that could backfire in ways she couldn't even begin to predict. But she had no choice. She had to know the truth.

—-

The following Saturday, Lila found herself standing in front of Nick's house once more. She had told herself she wasn't going to do this, that she wouldn't give in to the pressure. But somehow, here she was, standing at his door, rehearsing the words in her mind.

She had been avoiding him for the past few days, keeping her distance, but the opportunity was too tempting to pass up. She had to learn more about him, find out where his loyalties lay. If he was involved in whatever was happening with the inheritance, if he was connected to the people after it, then this was her chance to find out.

Taking a deep breath, Lila raised her hand and knocked on the door.

It took a moment, but then the door opened, and Nick stood there, his expression as pleasant as ever. His dark hair was slightly messy, and he wore a loose t-shirt and jeans. There was something about him that always made Lila feel like she was seeing the tip of an iceberg, the surface of something much deeper, much darker.

"Lila," he said with a smile that didn't quite reach his eyes. "I wasn't expecting you today. What brings you by?"

"I was in the neighborhood," she said, forcing a smile. "I thought I'd stop by and see how you were settling in. It's been a while since we had a proper chat."

Nick's smile remained, but there was a flicker of something unreadable in his eyes. "I'd be lying if I said I didn't appreciate the company," he said, stepping aside to let her in. "Come on in. I was just making coffee."

Lila hesitated, then stepped inside. The interior of Nick's home was even more sparse than before, the boxes still piled high, but there was something different about it now. The room felt colder, emptier, as if it had become more of a shell than a place to live. The furniture was basic, functional, and the walls were bare, except for a single framed photograph that caught Lila's eye. It was a picture of Matilda.

Her heart skipped a beat. It was an old photo, one she had never seen before. Matilda was smiling in the picture, standing next to a man Lila didn't recognize. They were in front of a large, imposing building, a mansion of sorts, with dark stone walls and large windows. The man was standing just a little too close to her aunt, his arm around her waist in a possessive manner. Lila didn't know who he was, but the picture made her uneasy.

It felt wrong.

"Who's that in the photo?" Lila asked, trying to sound casual.

Nick followed her gaze and then froze for a moment, his face flickering with something almost imperceptible. He quickly stepped forward, blocking her view of the picture. "Oh, that? It's just an old family photo," he said, a little too quickly. "Nothing important."

Lila nodded, but the suspicion gnawed at her. She couldn't help but feel that Nick was hiding something more than just the photo. She had to find out what it was, and she had to be careful not to let him see through her.

"So, coffee?" Nick said, trying to change the subject as he gestured to the kitchen. "It's the least I can do for such a surprise visit."

"Sure," Lila replied, keeping her tone light as she followed him into the kitchen. "I'd love some."

As he brewed the coffee, Lila sat at the small kitchen table, trying to gather her thoughts. She had to be careful. She had to keep her questions subtle, keep the conversation flowing naturally. She couldn't let him get suspicious.

"So, how have you been settling in?" Lila asked, trying to sound casual. "It's a nice neighborhood. A little quiet for my taste, but it has its charm."

Nick chuckled as he poured the coffee. "Yeah, it's quiet all right. A bit too quiet, maybe. But I'm getting used to it. It's peaceful here."

Lila leaned forward, her gaze steady. "Peaceful, huh? I think that's what everyone wants, isn't it? A little peace, a little quiet. But sometimes, too much peace can make you wonder what's really going on, don't you think?"

Nick turned sharply, his eyes locking with hers. For a moment, there was a flicker of something in his gaze—something dangerous. "I'm not sure I understand what you mean," he said, his voice low.

Lila's heart raced, but she forced herself to keep her expression neutral. "Oh, I just meant that people around here seem like they're keeping to themselves. Sometimes it's nice to have a little distraction, you know?"

Nick placed the coffee cups on the table and sat down across from her. The air between them had shifted, becoming charged with something unspoken. "You know," he said slowly, "I've been wondering about you, Lila. You seem like someone who knows more than she lets on. I can tell when people are hiding things."

Lila's stomach clenched at his words, but she didn't let it show. "Everyone has their secrets, don't they? I mean, what's life without a little mystery?"

Nick's smile was slow, calculating. "I'm not sure you're being entirely honest with me," he said softly, leaning in a little closer. "But that's okay. I can respect someone who knows how to keep things close."

Lila's pulse quickened. He was toying with her, pushing her buttons to see how far he could go. But she couldn't let him know that she was starting to crack. She had to stay calm. "I don't know what you mean," she said, trying to sound innocent.

Nick studied her for a moment, his gaze never leaving hers. "You know, I think we might be more alike than you realize. We both have a lot of secrets. And secrets, well… they have a way of coming out eventually."

Lila's blood ran cold. His words were a thinly veiled threat, one that made her realize just how dangerous this game was becoming. Nick wasn't just some curious neighbor. He was involved in something far darker than she had anticipated, and she was getting too close to the truth for comfort.

"I think it's time for me to go," Lila said abruptly, standing up. "I appreciate the coffee, but I've got some things to take care of."

Nick didn't try to stop her, but his smile was tight. "Of course, Lila. But remember, secrets have a way of slipping out. And when they do, it's never as pretty as you think it's going to be."

Lila forced a smile, though her heart was pounding in her chest. She turned and walked quickly out of the house, feeling Nick's eyes on her the entire way. As she stepped outside, she took a deep breath, trying to calm herself. She had learned something crucial today—Nick wasn't just a bystander in her life. He was a player. A dangerous one.

And now, Lila knew that she had to be more careful than ever.

Seven

Reveal

❧

The days that followed her unsettling conversation with Nick felt like an endless stretch of time, each moment dragging on longer than the last. Lila had tried to go about her days as usual, but every step she took seemed heavy, like she was walking through a fog of suspicion and doubt. Nick's words kept echoing in her mind, his cryptic remark about secrets lingering in the air, and his unwavering gaze that seemed to see through her. She couldn't shake the feeling that he was playing a game, and she was the unwitting pawn.

But the longer she avoided him, the more the tension grew. She had to confront the truth. Whatever game Nick was playing, whatever danger he was hiding, it was time to find out what it all meant. She couldn't keep circling around it forever.

And so, Lila made a decision. She would confront Nick. She

would find out what he knew, what he was hiding. No more guessing. No more waiting for the pieces to fall into place on their own. She was going to take control.

—-

It was late in the evening when Lila finally made up her mind. The air outside was crisp, the sky streaked with shades of purple and orange as the sun began to set. She had been pacing in her living room, her thoughts a storm of uncertainty, but now there was only resolve. She couldn't wait any longer.

Grabbing her coat, Lila stepped out of her apartment and into the street, her footsteps echoing in the empty night air. The streetlights cast long shadows, and as she walked toward Nick's house, she could feel her heartbeat quickening with every step. It wasn't fear she felt—it was a deep, gnawing need to uncover the truth, no matter the cost.

When she reached his house, she hesitated for a moment, her hand hovering above the doorbell. She didn't know what to expect once she walked inside. She didn't know how much Nick was involved in whatever had been happening, but she was about to find out.

With a deep breath, Lila pressed the doorbell.

The sound of the chimes rang through the quiet air, and for a few moments, everything seemed suspended in time. Then, the door opened, and there he was—Nick, standing in the doorway with that same calm, collected expression. But this time, there was something different in his eyes. Something darker.

"Lila," he said, his voice smooth, but there was an edge to it now, as if he knew exactly why she was standing there. "I wasn't expecting you."

"I need to talk to you," Lila said, her voice steady despite the nerves twisting inside her. She wasn't sure if she was ready for what was about to unfold, but she knew there was no turning back.

Nick stepped aside, allowing her to enter. "Come on in," he said, though there was something unsettling about the way he said it. Almost as though he had been expecting her.

Lila walked into the house, but this time, she noticed more details. The house was colder than before, the air thick with an oppressive silence. The boxes, the bare walls—they all seemed to be part of a carefully constructed facade. Nothing about this place felt like a home. It felt like a hideout.

Nick closed the door behind her, his movements deliberate. "What's on your mind, Lila?" he asked, his voice low, his eyes never leaving her face.

Lila turned to face him, trying to push down the anxiety that threatened to overwhelm her. "I need to know the truth," she said, her voice strong despite the uncertainty churning in her stomach. "About you. About my aunt. About everything."

Nick's eyes narrowed slightly, and for a brief moment, Lila saw something flash across his face—a flicker of recognition, like he had been expecting this moment. "You've been digging, haven't you?" he said, his tone casual, almost amused.

"I've been trying to figure out what you're hiding," Lila retorted, her voice rising with frustration. "I know you're not just some random neighbor. There's something more going on here. I don't know what you're involved in, but I'm done pretending I don't see it."

Nick's expression remained unchanged, but the air between them shifted. His posture, once relaxed, now became more tense. "You're right," he said, his voice darkening. "There's a lot more going on than you think. But you're asking questions you're not ready to hear the answers to."

Lila's heart hammered in her chest. "What do you mean? What's going on? What do you know about my aunt's estate? Why did she leave me everything? What's the connection between you and my aunt?"

Nick took a step closer, his eyes cold and calculating. "Your aunt wasn't just a quiet, eccentric woman. She was involved in something far bigger than you can imagine. She made enemies, Lila. Powerful enemies. And those enemies know about you now."

Lila's breath caught in her throat. "What do you mean? Enemies? I don't understand."

Nick's lips curled into a small, almost pitying smile. "You think it was just about money, don't you? About some inheritance? You've been playing catch-up, trying to figure out what Matilda left behind. But you're not asking the right questions."

He reached over and grabbed something from the table—a small, leather-bound notebook. He opened it, flipping through the pages until he stopped at a specific one. "This," he said, his voice heavy with meaning, "is what your aunt was trying to keep hidden. The inheritance wasn't just about wealth. It was about something much more valuable. Something that people would kill for."

Lila's heart stopped. "What are you talking about? What's in that notebook?"

Nick looked at her for a moment, his eyes gleaming with something dark and dangerous. Then, he set the notebook down and folded his arms across his chest. "I'm not going to tell you everything, Lila. Not yet. But I will say this—you're in over your head. You think you can handle this, but you have no idea what's at stake. There are people out there who would do anything to get what Matilda left behind. And you're the key to it all."

Lila's mind raced as she tried to make sense of his words. "Who are these people? Why are they after me?"

Nick's expression grew even colder. "They're the ones Matilda was trying to protect you from. The ones who wanted what she had. But she didn't give them everything. She made sure to keep the most important parts hidden. She left clues for you, Lila.

She wanted you to find them. But she also wanted you to be strong enough to face the consequences. To face them… when you found out."

Lila's hands trembled as she reached for the notebook, her mind barely able to process what Nick was saying. "I don't understand. I don't understand any of this."

Nick's eyes narrowed. "Matilda wasn't just a recluse. She was part of an underground network. A secret society, if you will. She had access to information—resources—that people would kill for. That's why she had to disappear. And that's why you're here. You're the one who's been chosen to take over her role. But there's a price, Lila. There's always a price."

Lila's thoughts swirled, each word he spoke sinking deeper into her mind, causing her to feel more lost and confused than ever before. A secret society? A network Matilda had been part of? What kind of world had her aunt been involved in? And why was she, of all people, now caught in the web of it?

"Nick," she said, her voice trembling, "I don't know what you're talking about. But I need to know more. I need to understand. I need to know what's really going on."

Nick's gaze softened just slightly, but the darkness in his eyes remained. "I know you do. But there's more to it than just knowing the truth. There's a choice you'll have to make, Lila. A decision that will change everything."

Lila swallowed hard, feeling the weight of his words pressing down on her chest. She didn't know how much more she could take. The secrets, the lies, the danger—it was all too much, too overwhelming. But there was one thing she knew for certain: she had to know the truth. No matter the cost.

"What's the choice?" she asked, her voice barely a whisper.

Nick stepped closer, his face inches from hers. "You'll have to choose, Lila. You can walk away from all of this. You can leave the estate behind, forget everything, and live the rest of your life in peace. Or… you can take what Matilda left behind and fight. Fight the people who will stop at nothing to get what they want."

Lila's heart pounded in her chest. The choice felt impossible, and yet it was one she couldn't avoid. She had no idea what the future held, but she knew she couldn't turn back now. The truth was within her grasp, and she was going to find it—no matter the cost.

Eight

Another Life

The weight of Nick's words hung in the air long after he had spoken them. Lila stood frozen in place, her thoughts swirling, her breath coming in shallow gasps. The notion that her aunt, Matilda, had been involved in something so much bigger than she had ever imagined felt like a betrayal of the life she had known. For years, she had been living in a world of quiet normalcy, running a small business, tending to her modest home, and keeping her distance from anything resembling danger. But now, standing in the cold, sterile interior of Nick's house, she was being thrust into a world she didn't recognize—a world of secrets, lies, and power struggles that reached farther than she could comprehend.

"You're lying," she whispered, but the words lacked conviction. Deep down, she knew Nick wasn't lying. She could feel the truth in his words, even though it was too monstrous to accept.

Nick's expression softened slightly, though his eyes still burned with an intensity that made her skin crawl. "I'm not lying, Lila. I'm telling you the truth. The only reason Matilda left you this inheritance was because you're the last piece of the puzzle. The last person who can finish what she started. You've been chosen, whether you like it or not."

Lila shook her head, her mind rejecting what he was saying. She wanted to believe that he was wrong, that there had to be some explanation that didn't involve secret societies or underground networks. But with every passing moment, the pieces of the puzzle were falling into place, and she couldn't unsee what was becoming more and more apparent. There was more to her aunt's life than anyone had ever let on, and now, she was standing at the center of it.

"What do you want from me?" Lila asked, her voice trembling despite her attempt to sound defiant. She wanted to demand answers, but fear was creeping into her thoughts, clouding her judgment. What if Nick was dangerous? What if this wasn't just about the inheritance, but something far more sinister?

Nick tilted his head slightly, his gaze never leaving hers. "I don't want anything from you, Lila. I'm here to help you. The people who are after you? They've been watching you. They've been watching this entire town. They'll stop at nothing to get what they believe is theirs. You're in the middle of something you don't understand yet, but you will. Soon."

Lila's heart pounded in her chest. The word watching echoed through her mind like a warning bell. It wasn't just the inheritance that was at risk—it was her life. She had become part of a game, a dangerous one, where the stakes were higher than she could have ever imagined.

"Who are these people?" she asked, her voice barely a whisper. "What do they want from me? From Matilda?"

Nick exhaled, the breath escaping slowly as though he was weighing his words carefully. "They want power, Lila. They've always wanted power. And Matilda was a key player in their game. She was one of them, but she wanted out. She wanted to protect you, which is why she left you everything she had. You're the heir to her legacy, whether you want it or not."

Lila took a step back, her mind reeling. "I'm not her heir," she said, trying to convince herself as much as him. "I'm just… just a woman trying to make a living. I don't want any part of whatever this is."

Nick's lips twisted into a small smile, though it didn't reach his eyes. "That's what Matilda thought too. But in the end, she couldn't walk away. No one can. Not once you've been pulled into this world. And now, you're in it. Whether you walk away or not, they'll come for you."

Lila's head was spinning. She could feel the walls closing in, the pressure mounting with every word Nick spoke. She had no choice but to accept that her aunt's life—her inheritance—was tied to something much darker. But even as her mind grasped for some semblance of control, she couldn't stop the rising tide of fear and uncertainty.

"I don't know what you expect me to do," Lila said, her voice shaking with frustration. "I don't know anything about these people, about any of this. I'm just a small-town woman. I don't belong in a world like this."

Nick took a step closer, his presence overwhelming. "You belong here now. You're not just some small-town woman. You're Matilda's blood. You're the key to unlocking what's been hidden for decades. And if you refuse to accept that, you'll pay the price."

The finality of his words settled over her like a cold blanket, and for a moment, Lila could only stand there, rooted to the spot, her mind unable to process the enormity of what he was saying. She was part of this world now, whether she liked it or not. Her aunt had left her a legacy—one that was tied to power, secrets, and a network of people who would do anything to control it. And the more she learned, the more she realized that there was no escape.

"I can't do this," she said, her voice a mixture of anger and fear. "I can't be a part of this world."

Nick looked at her, his expression unreadable. For a long moment, there was only silence between them. Lila could feel her pulse racing, the weight of her decisions pressing down on her with every passing second. She didn't know how to fight something this big, how to stand against people who had been working in the shadows for years. But she couldn't let them win. She couldn't let them take control of her life.

"You don't have a choice," Nick said softly, his voice suddenly serious. "It's already begun. You've already made your choice the moment you decided to uncover the truth."

Lila's heart skipped a beat. "What do you mean?"

Nick reached for the notebook again, flipping it open to a page marked with a red X. He slid it toward her across the table. "Matilda left a message. A clue, if you will. A way for you to understand what this is really all about. But you have to decide whether you want to know the truth."

Lila's hands shook as she picked up the notebook, her breath catching in her throat. The page in front of her was filled with cryptic symbols, phrases, and notes written in her aunt's unmistakable handwriting. It made no sense, but at the same time, it was clear that Matilda had been trying to communicate something important. Something urgent.

"Take it," Nick said. "But know this—once you understand what's written here, there's no going back."

Lila stared at the page for a long time, the symbols swirling in her mind, but they were more than just symbols. They were clues, and they were leading her somewhere. Leading her into a truth she wasn't sure she was ready to face. Her fingers traced the edges of the paper, the weight of the decision pressing heavily on her shoulders.

"I don't have a choice, do I?" Lila whispered, more to herself than to Nick.

Nick's gaze never left hers. "No. You don't."

With a trembling hand, Lila turned the page, her eyes scanning the words her aunt had written. The letters were jumbled at first, but then, a pattern began to emerge. She could feel the pieces falling into place, one by one. The symbols, the cryptic phrases—they weren't just random. They were instructions. And as her eyes moved down the page, a chill ran through her.

It was all connected. The inheritance, the underground society, the danger—everything. Her aunt had known what was coming. She had known that Lila would be drawn into this, that she would be the one to finish what Matilda had started.

Lila looked up from the page, her breath caught in her throat. "What now?" she asked, her voice barely audible.

Nick didn't respond immediately. Instead, he stood up and walked toward the window, looking out into the dark night. When he turned back to face her, his expression had softened, though his eyes remained cold. "Now, you start making your move. You fight. You take what's yours."

Lila's heart pounded in her chest. She didn't know how to fight in a world like this. She didn't know what to do next. But one thing was certain: she was no longer the woman she had been. She had crossed a line, and there was no turning back.

The truth had been revealed, and now, Lila had to decide what kind of woman she was going to become. She was in this world now, whether she was ready or not. And the only question left was whether she could survive it.

Nine

Connection

The following week felt like a whirlwind to Lila. Every time she thought she could sit down and process the enormity of her situation, another twist would come, pulling her deeper into a world she didn't understand. The inheritance, Matilda's secret life, the underground network—everything was becoming too complicated, too dangerous. But one thing was becoming clearer with each passing moment: Nick was more than just a neighbor. He was a player in this game. And she had become his unwilling co-conspirator.

The pages of Matilda's notebook still weighed heavily on her mind. The symbols, the cryptic messages—they didn't make sense, but they were part of something larger. They were instructions, and Lila was certain they were leading her somewhere, to something that would tie all of this together. What Matilda had left behind wasn't just a legacy of wealth—it was a carefully crafted plan, a blueprint that Lila now had to follow if she wanted to uncover the truth.

But how could she trust Nick? He had revealed part of the puzzle, but he had also made it clear that he wasn't giving her all the pieces. Every time she thought she was getting closer to the truth, he would retreat, pulling back just enough to keep her guessing. He was playing a game, and Lila wasn't sure whether she was winning or losing.

—-

It was late one evening when Lila received an unexpected call. Her phone buzzed as she sat at her kitchen table, staring at the pages of Matilda's notebook. She had spent the last few hours trying to decipher the symbols, but they still eluded her. There were patterns, yes, but they didn't form a coherent picture. Not yet.

She picked up the phone, and the familiar name on the screen made her stomach twist. Damon.

"Lila," Damon's voice was urgent, laced with tension. "We need to talk. Now."

Lila's pulse quickened. There was something in his tone that immediately set her on edge. "What's going on?" she asked, trying to keep her voice steady.

"Not over the phone," he said sharply. "Meet me at the café. I'll explain everything. It's about Nick. And Matilda's estate."

Lila's heart skipped a beat. Nick. Matilda's estate. Was Damon finally going to tell her everything she needed to know? Or was this just another piece of the puzzle that would send her deeper into a rabbit hole she couldn't escape?

"I'll be there in ten," she said, her voice shaking slightly as she hung up.

—-

The café was quiet when Lila arrived, the soft hum of conversation barely audible in the background. She spotted Damon immediately, sitting in the same booth they always used, his hands clasped together on the table. His face was drawn, his expression more serious than she had ever seen it before. Lila could tell that something was wrong, but she wasn't sure what.

"Damon," she said as she slid into the seat across from him. "What's going on? What did you want to tell me?"

Damon looked at her for a moment before speaking, his eyes scanning the room as though making sure no one was listening. "Lila, I've been doing some digging of my own," he began, his voice low. "I didn't want to bring this up until I had more information, but I think you need to know the truth. About Nick. About Matilda."

Lila's stomach tightened. She had known this conversation was coming, but hearing the words spoken aloud felt like a slap in the face. She had been living in a world of half-truths and lies, and now it seemed like the final pieces were about to fall into place.

"What do you know?" she asked, her voice barely above a whisper.

Damon took a deep breath. "Nick isn't just a random neighbor, Lila. He's connected to the people who've been tracking Matilda's estate. The people who've been watching you. And the worst part is, he's been manipulating you. He's not trying to help you, Lila. He's using you."

Lila's breath caught in her throat. She had suspected it, but hearing it from Damon made the truth hit her like a wave. "What do you mean, using me?" she asked, her voice shaking. "How?"

"He's trying to get you to lead him to something Matilda left behind," Damon explained, his eyes dark with concern. "Something that's tied to the estate. Something far more dangerous than you can imagine. I don't know the full details, but from what I've uncovered, it's not just about the money. It's about power. People will do anything to get their hands on it. And Nick is in the middle of it."

Lila felt a cold chill settle over her. "I thought he was helping me. I thought—" She stopped herself, realizing how naïve she had been. Everything Nick had said, every interaction they had shared, had been a calculated move on his part. He hadn't been helping her; he had been pulling her deeper into a game she didn't understand.

"I know this is a lot to take in," Damon said, his voice gentle now, as if he understood the turmoil she was feeling. "But you need to stay away from him. He's dangerous, Lila. And if you keep going down this path, you won't be able to get out."

Lila shook her head, the weight of everything crashing down on her. "I don't know what to do," she admitted. "I don't know who to trust. You, Nick… Matilda. Everything's a lie."

Damon reached across the table, his hand covering hers in a gesture of comfort. "I'm telling you this because I care about you, Lila. And because I'm worried about you. Nick has been playing both sides, and I think he's been using you to get closer to Matilda's secret. You need to make a choice, Lila. You need to choose what side you're on."

Lila's heart raced as she looked down at their hands, her mind spinning with the implications of Damon's words. She had trusted Nick, believed in the idea that he was just a man caught in the web of this dangerous inheritance. But now, she realized, she had been nothing more than a pawn in his game.

"I don't want to be a part of this anymore," she said, her voice firm, though there was a tremor in it. "I just want to walk away. I want to live my life without all of this."

Damon nodded slowly, his expression sympathetic but resolute. "I understand. But you can't just walk away, Lila. They won't let you. Not now that they know you're involved. Not now that you're the one who holds the key to everything."

Lila closed her eyes, the weight of his words sinking in. She had no choice but to keep going. She couldn't just walk away. Not when there was a mystery to unravel, not when she was already in so deep.

"I can't keep running from this," she whispered, her voice breaking. "I need to know the truth. I need to understand what Matilda left behind. What she was trying to protect me from."

Damon sighed, sitting back in his chair. "I can't stop you, Lila. But I'm telling you—whatever you think you know, it's just the tip of the iceberg. There's more to this than you can possibly imagine. And if you're not careful, you'll lose yourself in it."

Lila nodded, her resolve hardening. "I'm not going to let that happen. I'll finish what Matilda started. I'll uncover the truth, no matter the cost."

Damon studied her for a moment, as if weighing his options. "Be careful," he said finally. "You're in deeper than you realize. And Nick? He's not going to let you go that easily."

Lila stood up, the weight of her decision settling over her. The truth was out there, buried in the secrets Matilda had left behind. And she was going to find it. But the question was: could she survive what she would find once she did?

As she walked out of the café, the weight of her choices pressed down on her, but her determination was stronger than ever. The game was far from over, and she had just stepped into the darkest part of it.

Ten

Risky Proposal

Lila's mind raced as she walked home from the café, her heart still heavy with Damon's warning. He had told her the truth, or at least a part of it. Nick wasn't just a neighbor. He wasn't just a charming stranger offering to help her uncover her aunt's secrets. He was a part of something much darker, a player in a dangerous game. And she had unknowingly stepped right into the center of it.

Her thoughts felt like a whirlwind as she walked down the empty street, the cool night air doing little to clear the fog in her mind. What was she supposed to do now? Damon had been clear—Nick couldn't be trusted. He had used her to get closer to whatever it was Matilda had hidden. But what if Nick wasn't just a puppet in someone else's game? What if he was in this as deeply as the people he was working with?

The faint sound of footsteps behind her made her freeze. She turned, her eyes scanning the street for any sign of movement. The street was empty. Too empty. The hairs on the back of her neck stood on end as she quickened her pace. Was someone following her?

She rounded the corner, her heartbeat quickening with each step. The footsteps grew louder, closer. She didn't dare look back, but the feeling of being watched was undeniable. She was no longer just a woman trying to solve a mystery; she had become part of a much larger puzzle, one with pieces she couldn't even see.

As she approached her apartment building, a figure stepped out of the shadows, blocking her path.

Lila froze, her stomach dropping. "Nick," she said, her voice trembling despite herself. "What are you doing here?"

Nick's expression was calm, too calm. His eyes gleamed with something unreadable, a strange mix of satisfaction and calculation. "I think you know why I'm here, Lila," he said softly, his voice low and inviting, as if he were offering her something, something dangerous and irresistible. "We need to talk."

Lila swallowed hard. The last time they had spoken, things hadn't gone as planned. He had lied to her, manipulated her, and she had let him. She had let him get close, believing he was on her side. But now, she wasn't so sure. Now, she knew better than to trust him. But she also knew that walking away from him now, after everything she had learned, wasn't an option.

She had no choice but to face him.

"What do you want, Nick?" she asked, her voice firm, though she could feel the tremble in her hands. She could feel the weight of the choice pressing on her chest.

Nick smiled, a slow, deliberate smile that didn't reach his eyes. "I think it's time for you to make a decision, Lila. You've been dancing around the truth for long enough. You've been digging into Matilda's past, trying to understand what she left behind. But the truth is, you're not ready for it. You're not ready for what's coming."

Lila's heart pounded in her chest. "What's coming? What do you mean?"

Nick took a step closer, his presence overwhelming. "You're at a crossroads, Lila. You've uncovered part of the puzzle, but you've missed the most important pieces. There's a reason Matilda left you everything. You're the heir to her legacy. And whether you like it or not, you're already involved. You can't walk away from this. Not now."

Lila felt a chill run down her spine. He was right. She couldn't walk away. No matter how much she wanted to. The inheritance, the estate, the danger—everything was pulling her deeper into a world she didn't understand, a world she was trying to escape. But escape was no longer an option.

"I don't want any part of this," she said, her voice barely above a whisper. "I don't want to be a part of whatever this is."

Nick's eyes flickered with something like pity, but there was no warmth in his gaze. "You don't have a choice, Lila. You've already made your decision the moment you decided to dig into Matilda's life. You're in this, whether you like it or not."

Lila stepped back, her mind racing. "What do you want from me?" she asked, trying to keep her voice steady despite the storm swirling inside her. "Why are you here? What's your end game?"

Nick tilted his head, studying her with that calculating look she had come to dread. "I'm here to offer you a choice," he said, his tone as smooth as silk. "I can help you, Lila. I can help you unlock everything Matilda left behind. I can give you the answers you're looking for. But there's a price. You'll have to work with me. You'll have to trust me."

Lila's mind whirled. She had already trusted him once, and it had led her into a maze of lies and half-truths. What if he was telling the truth now? What if this was the only way to uncover the full extent of Matilda's secrets? She didn't have the luxury of time. The more she thought about it, the more she realized that Nick's offer might be the only chance she had to find out what was really going on. But what if it was a trap?

"What do you mean, 'work with you'?" Lila asked, her voice trembling despite her best efforts to sound composed.

Nick's smile widened, though there was no warmth in it. "You'll have to trust me, Lila. You'll have to join forces with me. Together, we can take control of what Matilda left behind. We can finish what she started."

Lila's breath caught in her throat. Take control. The words echoed in her mind, reminding her of everything she had uncovered so far—the secret society, the power struggles, the people who would stop at nothing to get what Matilda had hidden. Was Nick part of them? Was he working with them? Or was he playing both sides?

She couldn't tell, but she knew one thing for certain: her life, as she had known it, was over. No matter what she chose, no matter what path she walked, there was no going back.

"And what happens if I refuse?" Lila asked, her voice barely above a whisper.

Nick's eyes darkened, his expression hardening. "If you refuse, you'll be left in the dark. You'll never know the full truth. And worst of all, you'll be left exposed. The people who've been watching you? They'll come for you. They'll come for everything."

Lila felt the blood drain from her face. The fear that had been lurking in the back of her mind suddenly became a tangible, suffocating weight. If she refused Nick's offer, if she turned her back on everything she had uncovered, she would become a target. She would be hunted, just like Matilda had been. There was no escaping it.

"I don't have a choice, do I?" she whispered.

Nick's expression softened, though the darkness never left his eyes. "No, Lila. You don't."

For a long moment, the world seemed to stop. Lila's heart was pounding in her chest, and her thoughts were a blur. She had been thrust into this world unwillingly, and now she had to make a choice. A choice that would shape the rest of her life. She could walk away from it all and risk losing everything, or she could join forces with Nick, the man she had once trusted, and finish what Matilda had started.

"Okay," she said finally, her voice steady, though her hands trembled. "I'll work with you. But I need to know everything. No more secrets. No more lies."

Nick nodded slowly, a faint smile tugging at the corners of his lips. "You'll get everything you need, Lila. I promise. But remember this—once you step into this world, there's no turning back. You'll be in it for life."

Lila took a deep breath, her mind made up. She didn't know what the future held, but she knew one thing for certain: she was done hiding. She was done running. The truth was out there, and she was going to find it, no matter the cost.

Nick stepped aside, motioning for her to follow. "Come on. Let's get started. There's a lot to do, and we don't have much time."

As Lila followed him into the shadows, she couldn't help but wonder what kind of monster she was about to unleash. But it didn't matter. She had already made her choice. And now, there was no turning back.

Eleven

Trust

The room was dimly lit, the only source of light coming from a single, flickering lamp in the corner. Lila stood in the center of the room, her hands clenched at her sides, as she watched Nick pace back and forth. Her mind was racing, her heart hammering in her chest. The decision she had made to work with him felt like both a lifeline and a trap. She had been drawn into a world she didn't understand, a world where nothing was as it seemed. And now, there was no turning back.

Nick stopped pacing and turned to face her, his eyes locking with hers. His expression was unreadable, but there was a certain intensity in his gaze that made her feel exposed. He knew she was afraid. He knew she was uncertain. But that didn't matter. She had made her choice, and now, she had to live with it.

"I hope you're ready, Lila," Nick said, his voice low and steady. "What we're about to do isn't easy. It's going to test everything you've ever believed in. And it's going to test your trust in me."

Lila swallowed hard, trying to steady herself. She had no idea what she was about to get into, but she knew one thing: she couldn't back out now. Not after everything that had happened, not after everything she had learned. She had already come too far.

"I'm ready," she said, her voice firmer than she felt. "What do I need to do?"

Nick studied her for a moment, as though weighing her words, before nodding. "Good. First things first—we need to know where Matilda hid the key piece of the puzzle. The final piece. It's the one thing she kept hidden from everyone, even from me. And it's the one thing that will give us control over everything."

Lila's pulse quickened at the mention of the key piece. What could it be? What had Matilda hidden from the world? And why had she chosen to leave it to Lila? The questions were endless, but the answers were still out of reach.

"What is it?" she asked, her voice barely a whisper.

Nick walked over to a desk in the corner of the room and pulled out a small, worn envelope. He handed it to Lila, and she hesitated before taking it. The paper felt fragile in her hands, as though it had been handled many times before. She opened it carefully, her eyes scanning the contents. There was nothing inside except a single, folded sheet of paper.

She unfolded the paper, her hands trembling as she read the words that had been written in Matilda's unmistakable handwriting:

The key lies where the past and present meet. The truth is hidden in plain sight. Find the place where it all began, and you will find what you seek.

Lila frowned, her confusion mounting. What did it mean? The place where the past and present meet? It was a riddle, an enigma that made no sense. Matilda had left her a puzzle, one that seemed impossible to solve.

"Where do I start?" she asked, looking up at Nick.

Nick leaned against the desk, his arms crossed. "You start by thinking like Matilda. She wasn't a fool. She was a master at hiding things, at keeping the most important pieces of her life locked away. But she also had a love for old places, for history. If you want to find what she left behind, you need to understand her."

Lila looked down at the letter again, her mind racing. The past and present meeting. It could mean anything. She thought back to everything she knew about Matilda—the old house on the outskirts of town, the strange objects and trinkets Matilda had collected over the years, the way she had always seemed to know things before they happened. There was always a sense of mystery surrounding her aunt, a sense of knowing that Lila had never fully understood.

"You think it's at the house," Lila said slowly, her voice uncertain.

Nick's eyes flickered with something like approval. "Yes. I think it's there. But I also think you're not the only one who's looking. There are people who want what Matilda hid, and they've been watching you. They've been watching us. You can't go alone. You need to trust me, Lila. If you want to survive, you need to work with me."

Lila's mind raced, but something inside her told her that Nick was right. If she went alone, if she tried to figure this out on her own, she would be walking straight into a trap. She had already seen the shadows lurking around the edges of her life—people who would stop at nothing to get what they wanted. She couldn't afford to take that risk.

"I'll trust you," she said, her voice steady despite the fear that gripped her chest. "But I need to know everything. No more secrets. No more lies."

Nick's gaze softened, but only for a moment. "You'll get the truth, Lila. I promise. But you need to be prepared. This isn't going to be easy. Once we go to the house, once we start digging, there's no going back. We'll be exposed. And those who are after us won't hesitate to strike."

Lila nodded, steeling herself for what was to come. She had no choice but to trust him, even if every instinct in her screamed to run. There was no running from this. She had been caught in the web of Matilda's legacy, and the only way out was through it.

"Let's go," Lila said, her voice firm. "Let's find what she left behind."

—-

The drive to Matilda's house felt like an eternity. The world outside the car window blurred as Lila's thoughts swirled in a chaotic whirlwind. She had thought she knew the house—had spent countless afternoons there as a child, playing in the garden, exploring the rooms. But now, it felt different. The house, which had once been a place of comfort and warmth, now felt like a cold, oppressive monument to the secrets Matilda had kept.

Nick didn't speak much during the drive, his eyes focused on the road ahead, his expression unreadable. Lila didn't know what to expect once they arrived, but a small, nagging voice in her head told her that this was the point of no return. Once they stepped onto Matilda's property, once they started looking for the key piece, there would be no going back. The game would be over, and the real danger would begin.

When they arrived, the house loomed in front of them, the windows dark and lifeless. It looked abandoned, though Lila knew better. Matilda had kept the house in perfect condition, even in her final years. There was always something about the place that made it feel alive, as though it were waiting for something.

Nick got out of the car first, moving with a purpose. Lila hesitated for a moment, her hand on the door handle, before following him. The air was thick with the scent of damp earth and old wood, and the ground beneath her feet seemed to shift with every step.

"This way," Nick said, motioning toward the back of the house. Lila followed him, her heart pounding in her chest.

As they reached the rear door, Nick pulled out a key, unlocking the door with practiced ease. "Matilda always kept the back door unlocked," he said quietly. "She trusted me with the house. But trust is a dangerous thing, Lila. Trust can get you killed."

Lila nodded, her throat tight. She couldn't let fear control her now. She had come this far, and there was no turning back.

Inside, the house was exactly as she remembered it—dusty but familiar. The walls were lined with shelves of books and strange artifacts, each one more peculiar than the last. The faint smell of jasmine lingered in the air, a scent she had always associated with her aunt.

Nick moved toward the stairs, his movements purposeful. "We need to go upstairs," he said, his voice low. "The key piece is hidden in the place where Matilda's life began. She always said it was the only place she ever truly felt at home."

Lila followed him up the stairs, the old wood creaking beneath their feet. The upstairs was just as she remembered, the hallway lined with doors leading to the rooms where Matilda had lived, where she had kept her secrets.

Nick stopped in front of the last door on the left—the room where Matilda had kept her most cherished possessions. "This is it," he said, his voice barely a whisper.

Lila's heart skipped a beat. She had never been allowed in this room. It had always been locked, always off-limits. But now, standing in front of the door, she could feel the weight of the truth pressing down on her. Whatever was behind that door, whatever Matilda had hidden, was the final piece of the puzzle. And once she found it, her life would never be the same.

Nick turned the knob, and the door creaked open.

Lila stepped inside, her breath caught in her throat.

The room was filled with old trunks, dusty furniture, and shelves of books. But it was what lay in the center of the room that took her breath away.

There, on a pedestal, was an old, intricately carved box. It was covered in dust, but there was something about it—a quiet power that seemed to emanate from it, as though it were waiting for her.

Nick stepped forward, his eyes gleaming with anticipation. "This is it, Lila," he said, his voice low. "The key piece. The truth Matilda left behind. Now, it's time to open it."

Lila felt her heart race as she stepped forward, reaching out to touch the box. It was cold to the touch, its surface smooth and hard, but she could feel the weight of its significance. She had been led here, and now, it was time to uncover what was inside.

She took a deep breath and lifted the lid.

And as the box opened, the truth she had been searching for was finally revealed.

Twelve

True Motives

Lila's fingers trembled as they brushed across the inside of the box. It was as though she could feel the weight of a thousand secrets pressing against her hand, urging her to open it. The moment she had been waiting for had arrived—everything had led to this point. The inheritance, the lies, Nick's cryptic warnings, the strange symbols from Matilda's notebook—it all came down to this one moment, this one decision.

With a deep breath, Lila slowly lifted the lid of the box. The contents were hidden under a velvet cloth, the edges worn with age. She hesitated for a moment, her mind racing, before pulling the cloth aside.

The first thing she saw was a folded piece of yellowed paper. It was almost too small for the box, barely a few inches square, but it seemed to radiate an energy that made her pulse quicken. There was something about the way it was folded, as though it had been deliberately hidden, carefully kept from prying eyes.

Lila carefully unfolded the paper, her eyes scanning the hastily scribbled notes on the surface. The handwriting was familiar—it was Matilda's handwriting, but the words made no sense.

The truth will set you free, but it will also enslave you. Do not seek the answers until you are prepared to face the consequences. They will come for you. They have always been watching. Trust no one, not even me.

The cryptic words sent a shiver down Lila's spine. What did Matilda mean? What was she trying to warn her about? The note was filled with ominous phrases, each word more unsettling than the last. "They have always been watching." Who was Matilda talking about? The people who were after the inheritance? Or was there something more—something darker—lurking in the shadows?

Lila felt a cold sweat form on the back of her neck. Her eyes flickered back to the contents of the box. Beneath the paper, there were several small objects—old keys, a tarnished locket, and a faded photograph. She picked up the photograph first, feeling the weight of its history in her fingers. The image was of a young Matilda, standing with a man Lila didn't recognize. The man's arm was around her aunt's shoulders, a possessive grip, his face shadowed, his features barely visible. But it wasn't just the photo that caught her attention. It was the look in Matilda's eyes—fear, desperation, and something else—something that

Lila couldn't quite place.

Her heart hammered in her chest as she turned the photograph over. On the back, in faint pencil marks, was a name: Dante Voss. The name meant nothing to Lila. She had never heard of anyone by that name, but she knew it had to mean something. It had to be the key to unraveling the mystery Matilda had spent so much of her life hiding.

"Dante Voss," she whispered to herself, the name slipping off her tongue like a forgotten memory.

Nick, who had been standing silently behind her, stepped forward at the sound of the name. "Dante Voss," he repeated, his voice colder than before. "I was wondering when you'd figure that out."

Lila turned to face him, her heart skipping a beat. She hadn't heard him move, hadn't noticed the change in the air, but now, with his presence looming over her, everything felt different. The room seemed to shrink, the air thick with tension. Nick had always been mysterious, but now, she realized just how much he had been hiding. Just how deep his involvement went.

"You knew him?" Lila asked, her voice trembling. There was a sudden, terrifying realization in her mind—a sense that she had just uncovered something far darker than she could have imagined. "You knew Matilda's secret. You've known all along, haven't you?"

Nick didn't immediately respond, his eyes narrowing as he took a step closer. "You've been digging deeper than I thought," he said quietly. "But there's still a lot you don't understand."

Lila's breath caught in her throat. "Who was he? Who is he?" she demanded. "And why didn't you tell me?"

Nick's lips tightened into a thin line. "Dante Voss was the leader of a secret society—a network of powerful individuals who have been operating in the shadows for decades. They control everything, Lila. The money, the power, the influence. And Matilda was one of them."

Lila staggered backward, her mind reeling. "Matilda? She was involved in this—this society?" she gasped, struggling to comprehend the implications. "But why? Why would she get involved in something like that?"

Nick's eyes darkened, and he moved closer to her, his voice dropping to a whisper. "Matilda was a part of something far bigger than you know. She wasn't just some eccentric woman hiding away in her cottage. She was a key player in that society, and when she tried to break free, they came for her. She knew too much. She had to disappear."

Lila shook her head, the weight of Nick's words settling over her like a dark cloud. "And now they're coming for me," she whispered, as the realization hit her like a punch to the gut. "Because I'm the only one who can unlock what she left behind. They want me to finish what Matilda started."

Nick nodded slowly. "Exactly. They've been watching you, Lila.

Ever since you opened that box. They've known you'd find it. They've been waiting for you to unlock the secrets Matilda left behind."

Lila's chest tightened. She felt the walls of her world closing in on her, the noose tightening around her neck. She had been drawn into this dark game, and now there was no way out. But what could she do? The people who were after her aunt were coming for her now. And they wouldn't stop until they had what they wanted.

"I don't know what to do," Lila whispered, her voice breaking. "I can't fight them. I don't know how."

Nick's gaze softened, though there was still an edge of something cold in his eyes. "You don't have to fight them alone. That's why I'm here. I've been part of their world for a long time, Lila. I know how they think. I know how to play the game. I can help you."

Lila looked up at him, the weight of his words pressing down on her. She had trusted him before, and now, in the wake of this revelation, she didn't know if she could trust him again. He had been a part of this world all along—he had known what she was getting into, and yet he had allowed her to walk into it blindly. Was he on her side? Or was he just using her to get what he wanted?

"I don't know if I can trust you anymore," Lila said, her voice barely above a whisper. "I don't know if I can trust anyone."

Nick's expression hardened, his jaw clenched. "I understand your hesitation. But you don't have a choice. The people who want what Matilda hid—they won't stop. They'll come for you, Lila. They'll destroy everything in their path to get what they want. And if you want to survive, you need to trust me. You need to trust that I can protect you."

Lila's mind raced as she considered his words. The darkness surrounding her seemed to close in on her from all sides, suffocating her. She had no choice but to trust Nick, at least for now. But the questions lingered—was he truly on her side, or was he just another piece in a game that she didn't understand? And what was it that Matilda had left behind? What was the key piece that everyone was fighting for?

She looked down at the box again, her fingers tracing the edges of the photograph. Dante Voss. A secret society. The key piece. All of it was connected, but how? And what was she supposed to do with the information she had now?

Nick's voice broke through her thoughts. "You're not alone in this, Lila. You can trust me."

Lila met his gaze, the weight of her decision pressing down on her. She didn't know who to trust. She didn't know what the truth was anymore. But one thing was certain: she was deeper in this than she had ever intended to be. And the only way out was to keep moving forward.

"Alright," she said, her voice steady, though her heart raced with fear. "I'll trust you. But if you lie to me again, Nick, I swear I'll never trust you again."

Nick nodded, his expression serious. "I won't lie to you, Lila. I promise. Together, we'll finish what Matilda started. Together, we'll uncover the truth."

And with those words, Lila knew that there was no turning back. She had entered a world of shadows, and now, she had no choice but to keep moving through them. But the question remained— would she survive the darkness? Or would it consume her like it had consumed so many before her?

Thirteen

Healing

The morning light filtered through the cracks in the curtains, casting a pale, ghostly glow across the room. Lila awoke with a start, her body stiff and her mind still tangled in the web of confusion and fear that had taken root in her life. The events of the last few days played in her mind like an endless loop: the hidden inheritance, the cryptic messages from Matilda, the unsettling truth about Nick, and the dark world she had been pulled into. She felt like she was drowning in it all, gasping for air but unable to break free.

She sat up slowly, her hands rubbing her temples in an attempt to ward off the headache that had been gnawing at her since the night before. The conversation with Nick had left her feeling exhausted, both physically and emotionally. He had been right about one thing—there was no turning back now. She had entered a world of shadows and secrets, and she had no idea how to navigate it.

But there was something else gnawing at her—a feeling of deep loss, of betrayal, and of heartbreak. How had everything gone so wrong? She had trusted Nick, believed in his promises, and now, she felt like a fool. The man who had once seemed like her ally, the one who had offered to help her unlock the secrets of her aunt's past, was now a stranger—someone whose motives were unclear, whose true intentions seemed to shift with every passing moment.

Lila stood and walked to the window, staring out at the world outside. The morning sun illuminated the street below, but it did little to brighten the darkness that had settled in her heart. Everything had been turned upside down. Matilda's legacy, the inheritance, the strange society, Nick—none of it was what she had expected. None of it was simple. It was all tangled up in lies, betrayal, and power struggles that she had never imagined.

Her phone buzzed on the nightstand, cutting through her thoughts. She glanced at the screen, her stomach tightening when she saw the name. Damon. She hadn't spoken to him since their last meeting, where he had warned her about Nick and everything that was unfolding. He had seemed so certain, so steadfast in his belief that Nick was using her. But was Damon right? Or had she misjudged everything?

Taking a deep breath, Lila reached for the phone and answered.

"Lila," Damon's voice came through, calm but with a hint of urgency. "We need to talk."

Lila's chest tightened. "I know," she said quietly. "I've been thinking a lot about what you said. About Nick. I don't know what to believe anymore, Damon."

"I know," Damon replied. "But we have to move quickly. The people who are after you are closing in. You don't have much time."

Lila's breath caught in her throat. "What do you mean? What's happening? What do you know?"

"I've been getting reports," Damon said. "People are starting to ask questions. About you. About the inheritance. They know you're connected to Matilda's estate, and they won't stop until they have everything. You're in danger, Lila. More than you know."

Lila's mind raced. She had known this was coming, had felt the threat lurking in the background, but hearing Damon's words made it real—too real. The danger was no longer distant. It was here. It was now.

"I don't know what to do," Lila whispered. "I don't know who to trust."

Damon's voice softened, as if sensing her fear. "You can trust me, Lila. I've always been here for you. But this isn't something you can face alone. You need to make a choice. You need to decide what kind of life you want to lead. You can keep fighting, keep digging, or you can walk away and live in peace. But I won't let you face this without knowing what you're up against."

Lila felt a lump form in her throat. She wanted to believe Damon, wanted to trust him with everything in her heart. But what about Nick? He had been there, too. He had been the one to promise to help her, the one to lead her down this path. And now, with everything coming to a head, she didn't know if she could keep walking beside him. She didn't know if she could keep trusting him.

"I don't know if I can do this anymore," she said, her voice breaking. "I don't know if I'm strong enough."

Damon's silence on the other end of the phone was heavy, filled with understanding and concern. "Lila," he said finally, his voice gentle but firm. "I know it feels like the weight of the world is on your shoulders right now. I know it feels impossible, like everything is falling apart. But you are stronger than you think. You've always been strong. And if you want to find the truth, if you want to protect yourself, you have to keep fighting. You can't let the darkness win."

Lila closed her eyes, trying to breathe through the sudden rush of emotion. Damon was right. She had always been strong. She had built her life from the ground up, fought for everything she had, and she couldn't let fear take it all away. She couldn't let the lies and the uncertainty swallow her whole. She had to fight back.

"Okay," she said, her voice steady now. "I'll do it. I'll find out the truth. I'll stop running."

Damon's voice softened. "You're not alone in this, Lila. I'm with you, every step of the way."

Lila nodded, even though she knew he couldn't see her. "Thank you," she whispered.

As she hung up, Lila took a deep breath, feeling a flicker of hope ignite in her chest. She wasn't alone. Damon was right. She didn't have to do this by herself. She could trust him, at least for now. But what about Nick? What about the promises he had made? What about the trust she had placed in him?

She couldn't afford to waste time second-guessing. The people after her, the people after Matilda's legacy—they were closing in. And she had a choice to make. She could keep trusting Nick, keep moving forward in the dark, or she could follow Damon's advice and face this head-on with the knowledge she had. The truth. The key piece that Matilda had left behind.

Lila felt a deep sense of resolve settle over her. She had chosen to keep going. She had chosen to face the truth, no matter how painful or dangerous it might be. But as she stood there, alone in her apartment, she couldn't shake the nagging feeling that the hardest part of all was yet to come. The real test wasn't finding the truth. It was living with it.

—-

Hours later, Lila found herself standing in front of Matilda's house once more. The place still felt like a ghost, empty and abandoned, despite everything that had happened there. She hadn't expected to feel the weight of her decision so heavily, but as she stood there, the sense of loss and betrayal hung over her.

The door creaked open, and Nick stepped out, his expression unreadable. For a moment, the two of them stood facing each other, the distance between them feeling wider than ever. Nick's eyes searched her face, as though waiting for some sign of what she had decided.

"I didn't think you'd come back," he said finally, his voice tinged with something she couldn't quite place.

Lila took a step forward, her heart pounding in her chest. She didn't know what to say. She didn't know if she could trust him anymore. But she had made her choice. She had made her decision.

"I'm here," she said, her voice firm. "But we need to talk. About everything. No more lies."

Nick nodded, his gaze darkening. "I understand. But know this, Lila. The truth isn't always what you want it to be."

Lila's chest tightened as the weight of his words settled over her. She had spent so much time searching for answers, but now, as she stood on the precipice of everything she had ever known, she realized that finding the truth might be the most dangerous thing of all.

As they walked inside together, Lila knew that everything was about to change. The road ahead was uncertain, and the people who were after her were closing in. But she was ready. Ready to face the truth. Ready to face whatever came next.

The hardest part was yet to come, but she wasn't going to run. Not anymore.

Fourteen

Final Decision

The house felt like a mausoleum as Lila stepped inside. The familiar, musty smell of old wood and dust clung to the air, yet there was a palpable tension in the space—a heaviness that hadn't been there before. Matilda's presence, once so deeply ingrained in the house's bones, seemed to have vanished, leaving only echoes behind. Lila ran her fingers over the dusty banister, feeling the roughness beneath her fingertips, as if touching something long forgotten. This house, this place, had once been home to so many secrets. And now, standing here, Lila realized that it was her turn to uncover them.

Nick stepped in behind her, closing the door with a soft click that echoed through the silence. He didn't speak at first, his gaze flicking over the familiar surroundings, as if searching for something. Lila couldn't tell if he was searching for answers or waiting for her to make the next move. His expression was guarded, his eyes sharp and calculating, but there was something else there too—something that made her wonder whether he was as caught up in this as she was.

"Are you sure about this?" Nick asked, his voice low, almost hesitant. "You know what this means. Once you make this choice, there's no going back."

Lila nodded, her throat tight. She had asked herself that question a thousand times over the past few days. She had thought about it all—the danger, the uncertainty, the people who would stop at nothing to get what Matilda had left behind. But as she stood here, in the house where her aunt had once lived, she felt something stir deep inside her. A sense of purpose. A sense of destiny. This was her path now. She had no choice but to walk it.

"I don't have a choice, Nick," she said, her voice steady despite the storm that was raging inside her. "I can't keep running. I have to know the truth. I have to finish what Matilda started."

Nick's eyes darkened as he studied her. "And you're ready to face the consequences?"

Lila took a deep breath, feeling the weight of his words sink into her. Was she ready? The thought of everything she had uncovered so far—the secret society, the inheritance, the people who were watching her, waiting for her to unlock the last piece of the puzzle—was overwhelming. But this was her moment. The moment that would define everything.

"I have to be," she whispered.

Nick didn't reply immediately. Instead, he walked past her, moving deeper into the house. Lila hesitated for a moment, her heart pounding in her chest. She knew what this was—this was the point of no return. Everything she had learned, everything she had uncovered, had led her here. There was no turning back.

With a final glance around the room, Lila followed Nick, her footsteps echoing in the silence as they ascended the staircase to the upper floor. The house felt different now, colder. Each step felt heavier, as though the weight of the decisions she had made was settling onto her shoulders. She could feel the eyes of her aunt on her, the silent judgment of a woman whose secrets were about to be exposed.

Nick stopped in front of the door to Matilda's room, the door Lila had never been allowed to open as a child. It had always been a place of mystery, a place Lila had been told to stay away from, and yet here she was, standing in front of it, with the key to its mysteries in her hand.

"This is it," Nick said softly, his voice carrying a note of finality. "Everything you've been searching for, everything that's been hidden, is behind this door."

Lila nodded, swallowing hard. She reached out, her fingers brushing against the old, weathered handle. The door creaked as she turned it, the sound somehow louder than it should have been. It was as though the house itself was holding its breath.

The room was just as Lila remembered it—dark, full of shadows, with the faint scent of jasmine lingering in the air. The furniture was covered with white sheets, and the windows were closed, casting the room in a dim, sepia-toned light. But it wasn't the room itself that caught Lila's attention. It was what was in the center of the room—on the floor, covered by a velvet cloth.

Lila's heart raced as she stepped forward, her fingers trembling as she lifted the cloth. Beneath it was a small, intricately carved wooden box, its surface worn and aged, the edges soft from years of handling. This was it. This was the final piece of the puzzle.

Nick stood behind her, watching her closely, his presence heavy and silent. "Go ahead," he said softly. "Open it."

With a deep breath, Lila placed her hands on the box, lifting it carefully. She could feel the weight of it, the significance of what it represented. This was the key to everything—the secret Matilda had kept hidden from the world. And now, it was in her hands.

She took another breath, then slowly opened the box.

Inside, there were more papers—parchments that looked ancient, faded with time. But there was also a small, delicate locket, its gold surface shining faintly in the low light. The locket was familiar. Lila had seen it before—Matilda had worn it often, and it had always seemed like more than just a piece of jewelry. It had seemed like something important, something powerful.

Lila reached for the locket first, her fingers brushing against the cool metal. She turned it over in her hands, her heart pounding as she tried to steady herself. There was an engraving on the back, and when she turned it toward the light, she could just make out the faded letters: Dante Voss.

The name sent a shiver down her spine. The man in the photograph, the man Matilda had once known, the man who had been a part of the secret society that had controlled everything. The locket was a symbol, a token, a connection between Matilda and the man who had been at the heart of everything.

Lila opened the locket carefully, her fingers trembling. Inside, there was a small, faded photograph—one of Matilda, but this time, she was standing next to a man. It wasn't the same man as in the earlier photo, but this one had the same cold, calculating eyes. This man's face was sharper, more defined, but there was something familiar about him. Lila felt a chill as she recognized the man.

Dante Voss.

And then, a letter fell from inside the locket. It was fragile, yellowed with age, and covered in Matilda's familiar handwriting. With trembling hands, Lila unfolded the letter, her eyes scanning the words as they swam before her vision:

They have always been watching. They will never stop until they have everything. The key to their power lies with me, and now, with you. I've made a terrible mistake by involving myself with them. And now, I'm afraid it's too late. But you must understand, Lila. They will come for you. I've left a trail—follow it, and you will uncover the truth. But be careful. The price of this truth is higher than you can imagine.

Lila's breath caught in her throat as she read the final words. She could feel the weight of Matilda's warnings sinking into her bones, her aunt's fears becoming her own. She had been right. Matilda had known exactly what she was doing when she left Lila the inheritance. She had known the danger, and she had hoped, perhaps in vain, that Lila would be able to carry on the fight.

Nick stepped forward, his voice low, almost reverent. "The truth is always more dangerous than we think, Lila. But it's the only way to end this. To stop them. You're the key to everything."

Lila looked at him, her heart racing, her mind spinning. She had thought she was ready for the truth, but now that she had it in her hands, now that she could feel the weight of it pressing down on her, she wasn't so sure.

The truth would change everything. But could she survive it?

Could she survive what came next?

The decision hung in the air, the silence stretching between them like a chasm, as Lila realized that the final choice was hers. Would she take control of her fate? Or would the shadows of the past swallow her whole?

She had to decide. And in that moment, as the weight of the locket pressed against her palm, Lila knew that the hardest part of all was not uncovering the truth—it was facing the consequences of the choice she was about to make.

The choice that would shape her future, and perhaps, the fate of everyone she loved.

She took a deep breath, and with trembling hands, closed the box.

Fifteen

Betrayal Unveiled

The weight of the box felt heavy in Lila's hands, but not because of the objects it contained. It was the weight of the truth that lay hidden within its corners—the truth she had long sought but now wasn't sure she was ready to confront. The locket, the letter, and the photograph had revealed fragments of a story, a story Matilda had carried with her until the day she died. It was a story that tied her to a powerful, dangerous network—a secret society that had watched her, controlled her, and, in the end, had manipulated her.

But Lila could feel something else settling in her gut as she stood there in the dim room, the silence pressing down on her. Betrayal. The kind of betrayal that hit deeper than any secret could, because it was not just about trust—it was about everything she had believed in. About everything she thought she understood.

Matilda had not only hidden the truth from the world—she had hidden it from Lila, too. The inheritance, the cryptic messages, the hidden pieces of a puzzle that Matilda had left for Lila to uncover, were all part of a plan. A plan Lila now knew had been devised to lead her to this moment, to the truth that was far darker than anything she could have ever imagined.

And Nick… He had been there, hadn't he? A part of it all. A part of the network Matilda had been a part of. But how much did he know? How much of what he had told her was truth, and how much was a lie designed to manipulate her?

Lila closed her eyes, the smell of jasmine from the room's air, the faint scent of nostalgia that still lingered from Matilda's days of living here, mixing with the acrid scent of betrayal in the air. She had trusted Nick, believed his promises of help, but everything she had discovered in the past few days had turned him into something else. Something far more dangerous.

"Why didn't you tell me everything, Nick?" Lila's voice broke the silence, the words coming out in a whisper that barely reached him. But her gaze was piercing, her eyes locked on him, trying to find any shred of honesty in the man who had become both her ally and her enemy.

Nick stood at a distance, his face as unreadable as ever. His eyes met hers with a cold, calculated look, but there was something else—a flicker of regret, maybe, or was it something else?

"You know why, Lila," he said, his voice low and smooth. "You weren't ready to know. If I had told you everything, you wouldn't have been able to handle it. No one can. Not even Matilda."

Lila's heart pounded in her chest as she absorbed his words. Not even Matilda.

The truth she had been seeking had always been more than just about her aunt's secrets. It had always been about power, control, and the men and women who pulled the strings from the shadows. Matilda had been a part of it, and now Lila was stuck in the same web.

"I don't care about your reasons anymore, Nick," she said, her voice trembling. "You used me. You lied to me. You were never trying to help me. You were just trying to get closer to whatever it is Matilda left behind. Whatever you've been hiding, I'm done being a part of it."

Nick's expression darkened, and for a moment, the calm, collected persona slipped away, revealing something colder, more dangerous beneath the surface. "You think you have a choice?" he asked, his tone sharp. "You think you can just walk away from this? From them?"

Lila's pulse quickened. She stepped forward, clutching the box in her hands, feeling the weight of it, the weight of everything that had happened. "Yes, I can. I'm not like you. I'm not a part of this world. I won't let you drag me into it any more."

Nick's face hardened, and for a moment, Lila saw something in his eyes—something almost desperate. But then, it was gone, replaced by that cold, calculating expression. "You think you can just walk away from all of this?" he repeated. "That's what Matilda thought, too. She thought she could leave. But no one leaves. Once you're in, you're in for life."

The words echoed in Lila's mind, each one sinking deeper into her chest. No one leaves.

But why had Matilda tried to protect her, then? Why had she left her the inheritance? Why had she gone to such great lengths to shield Lila from this world, if she knew there was no escape?

Lila shook her head, feeling a wave of anger rising inside her. "I'm not like her, Nick. I'm not going to stay in this twisted game. I don't care what you've been involved in. I won't be a part of it anymore."

Nick's lips twisted into a smile, but there was no warmth in it. "You're wrong," he said softly. "You've been a part of it from the beginning, Lila. You just didn't know it yet. The moment you found that box, you were already in. You're part of this, whether you accept it or not."

A chill ran down Lila's spine as his words sunk in. She had been part of it all along, hadn't she? The inheritance wasn't just money—it was a key to something much darker. Something that had been set in motion long before she ever walked into Matilda's life.

Nick stepped closer, his eyes locking with hers. "But you don't have to face this alone. We could be a team, Lila. Together, we could finish what Matilda started. We could take control of the network. You could have everything you ever wanted."

Lila stepped back, shaking her head. "You think I want this?" she spat, her voice rising. "You think I want any part of your twisted world? I want nothing to do with it, Nick. I just want to live my life in peace."

Nick's expression faltered for a moment, but only for a moment. His face quickly hardened again, his eyes cold. "You're naive, Lila. You can't escape it. They'll come for you, and when they do, you'll have nowhere to hide. You'll wish you had trusted me."

"I'm not afraid of you," Lila snapped. "I'm not afraid of anyone anymore."

For a moment, the room was silent, the only sound the faint creak of the floorboards beneath their feet. The tension between them was palpable, the air thick with unspoken words, unshed feelings. But in that silence, Lila realized something. She wasn't afraid. Not of Nick. Not of the people chasing after her. She had been afraid, yes—but that was before she knew the truth. That was before she realized that she had the power to make a choice.

She didn't have to stay trapped in this world. She didn't have to accept Nick's version of reality.

"I don't need you, Nick," she said, her voice steady now. "I'm done with your lies, your manipulation. This ends now."

Nick's eyes flashed with something cold, something dangerous, but Lila didn't flinch. She was done with him, with everything he represented. She would face the truth, but on her terms. She would uncover the rest of Matilda's secrets, but she wouldn't let herself be consumed by them. Not anymore.

Nick took a step back, his jaw tightening, but he said nothing. The silence that followed was almost unbearable, but Lila stood firm. She wasn't backing down.

The battle wasn't over—not yet. But Lila had made her decision. She would fight. She would uncover everything Matilda had hidden. But she would do it alone, without Nick's lies and without anyone trying to control her.

With a final look at him, Lila turned and walked away, the weight of the box still heavy in her hands, but the burden in her heart lifting. She wasn't alone. Not anymore.

The path ahead was still unclear. The danger was still very real. But Lila had found something that had been missing for a long time: hope. And with that hope, she knew she had the strength to face whatever came next.

The betrayal had been unveiled. But now, it was time for Lila to choose her own fate. And this time, no one—no matter how powerful, no matter how manipulative—could stop her from claiming it.